D1429263

THE HONOURS OF SCOTLAND

THE HONOURS
OF SCOTLAND

THE STORY OF
THE SCOTTISH CROWN JEWELS
AND THE STONE OF DESTINY

CHRIS TABRAHAM

Published in 2019 by Historic Environment Scotland
Enterprises Limited SC510997

Text updated and expanded from *The Honours of Scotland: The Story of the
Scottish Crown Jewels* and *The Stone of Destiny: Symbol of Nationhood*
published by Historic Scotland

HISTORIC   ÀRAINNEACHD
ENVIRONMENT   EACHDRAIDHEIL
SCOTLAND   ALBA

Historic Environment Scotland
Longmore House
Salisbury Place

Edinburgh EH9 1SH

Registered Charity SC045925

British Library Cataloguing-in-Publication Data. A catalogue record for this
book is available from the British Library.

ISBN 978 1 849172 75 2

Typeset in Trajan and Minion

Proofread by Ten Thousand Publishing Services

Indexed by Linda Sutherland

Printed in Slovenia by Imago

MIX
Paper from
responsible sources
FSC   FSC® C005748

CONTENTS

The Honours of Scotland

On 4 February 1818, a distinguished group of men gathered on the stair outside the Crown Room in Edinburgh Castle. Standing beside the Lord President of the Court of Session, the Lord Justice Clerk, the Lord Chief Commissioner of the Jury Court, the Lord Provost of the City of Edinburgh and the Commander-in-Chief of the Army was an anxious Walter Scott, one of Scotland's foremost authors and antiquarians. His urgent pleas to the Prince Regent (the future King George IV) had resulted in a royal warrant permitting Scott to accompany the Scottish Officers of State to open the sealed Crown Room in search of the Scottish Crown, Sceptre and Sword of State, known as the Honours of Scotland.

The group watched in silence as the masonry blocking was removed from the doorway. In the darkness beyond they spied a great iron-bound oak chest. They approached with great apprehension, for there was a suspicion that the chest was empty. The Honours had been locked away in 1707 following the Treaty of Union with England but many believed that ceremony had been a hoax.

One of the two padlocks which was broken as the oak chest was forced open to reveal the Honours, the Scottish Crown Jewels, which had been hidden away for over one hundred years.

Let Walter Scott himself describe what then happened:

*The chest seemed to return a hollow and empty
sound to the strokes of the hammer, and even those
whose expectations had been most sanguine felt
at the moment the probability of disappointment
… The joy was therefore extreme when, the
ponderous lid of the chest being forced open,
the Regalia were discovered lying at the bottom
covered with linen cloths, exactly as they had
been left in the year 1707 … The reliques were
passed from hand to hand, and greeted with
the affectionate reverence which emblems so
venerable, restored to public view after the slumber
of more than a hundred years, were so peculiarly
calculated to excite. The discovery was instantly
communicated to the public by the display of the
Royal Standard, and was greeted by shouts of
the soldiers in the garrison, and a vast multitude
assembled on the Castle Hill; indeed the rejoicing
was so general and sincere as plainly to show
that, however altered in other respects, the people
of Scotland had lost nothing of that national
enthusiasm which formerly had displayed itself in
grief for the loss of these emblematic Honours, and
now was expressed in joy for their recovery.*

Sir Walter Scott, famous novelist and antiquarian, was central
to the rediscovery of the Honours in Edinburgh Castle.

No one can have been more overjoyed than Scott himself. And the drama of that February morning proved a fitting climax to the fascinating and eventful story of the Honours of the Kingdom, a story which begins in the Dark Ages, takes us through the glory of Scotland's medieval history and reaches right up to the present day, with the Honours on display in the Crown Room at Edinburgh Castle.

CHAPTER 1
SCOTLAND AND KINGMAKING

On New Year's Day in the year 1651, Charles II was crowned King of Scots in the tiny church beside Scone Palace by Perth. It proved to be the last coronation there, and indeed the last in Scotland.

Many a king before Charles had been enthroned at Scone, traditionally the place of inauguration of Pictish kings since at least the seventh century. A glittering array of monarchs, including Macbeth, Malcolm Canmore, John Balliol and Robert the Bruce, had all journeyed to the ancient mound, the Moot Hill, to declare publicly their acceptance of the rights and obligations of kingship, to receive the symbols of sovereignty and accept the homage of their loyal subjects.

On that Ne'er Day in 1651, the young Charles II was mantled in royal robes and presented with the 'Honores of Scotland': the Crown, Sceptre and Sword, together with a pair of Spurs. These are the Honours of Scotland which are today displayed in the Crown Room in Edinburgh Castle. They date from the reign of King James IV (1488–1513) and his son King James V (1513–42). But the tradition of inaugurating new sovereigns with symbols of power such as crowns, sceptres and swords reaches far back into antiquity.

A nineteenth-century engraving of Charles II's crowning in 1651. This coronation, at the traditional royal power centre of Scone, was the last to take place in Scotland.

THE ANCIENT KINGS OF SCOTS

Our earliest reference to a royal inauguration dates back to the year 574 and takes us to Iona, or Io, the tiny speck of land off the coast of Argyll where St Columba – Colum Cille, 'Dove of the Church' – founded his monastery in around 563 and in so doing created Scotland's spiritual home of Christianity. Iona was where the first kings of Scots were inaugurated and where many of them were laid to rest, including Macbeth in 1057.

In 574, it is written, an angel appeared to Columba and commanded him to ordain Áedán mac Gabhráin King of the Scots of Dál Riata. According to Adomnán, Columba's biographer:

> *The saint, in obedience to the command of the Lord, sailed across to the island of Io and there ordained, as he had been commanded, Áedán to be King, who had arrived at the same time as the saint. During the words of consecration, the saint declared the future regarding the children, grandchildren and great-grandchildren of Áedán, and laying his hand upon his head, he ordained and blessed him.*

This is the first tantalising glimpse we have of the inauguration ceremony of a Scottish king. There is no mention either of crowning or of anointment; just the simple act of ordination, the 'laying on of hands', by the holy man Columba.

This 1920s stained-glass window by Douglas Strachan in St Margaret's Chapel, Edinburgh Castle, depicts St Columba, the first recorded ordainer of a Scottish king.

A further clue to the nature of the ceremony is given by Cumméne the White, the seventh Abbot of Iona, who recorded that the saint began to prophesy by saying to King Áedán:

Charge your sons that they also shall charge their sons and grandsons and descendants, not through evil counsels to lose their sceptre of this kingdom from their hands.

In Dark Age Scotland, as elsewhere in Europe, kings like Áedán, who ruled over a people recently arrived from Ireland, and the kings of the native-born Picts, were more like tribal warlords who exacted tribute from the peoples in their territory and led raiding parties beyond it. But through the Middle Ages, the nature of kingship changed. As the nations of Europe emerged, along with the Christianisation of the West, so too did the medieval tradition of enduring royal power, and the instantaneous transfer of sovereignty from the dead monarch (the 'body natural') to their successor (the 'body politic') – whence the acclamation: 'The King is Dead! Long Live the King!' The act of coronation became a ritual confirmation of sovereignty that had already been transferred, and crowns, sceptres, orbs and swords became important tangible and visible symbols of that sovereignty.

The sceptre and orb signified the sacred nature of kingship, bestowing an authority to rule with discretion and sincerity, not with tyranny and partiality. The Sword, on the other hand, was a symbol of power on earth, imposing on its holder a duty both to dispense justice and to protect his subjects from their enemies.

About 842, Kenneth mac Alpin (Cináed mac Alpín), already King of the Scots, also became King of the Picts. Thus the nature of kingship changed. The Scottish royal house was transformed from a remote Irish warband controlling Argyll from its rock-fast fortresses at Dunadd and elsewhere into a powerful dynasty controlling a greater part of northern Britain from the ancient Pictish base at Scone, beside the River Tay, near Perth. Dark Age Dunadd, rising from the broad floodplain of Mòine Mhór, 'the Great Moss', has intriguing carvings near its summit, including a sunken footprint, a rock-cut basin and the incised outline of a wild boar. Could they perhaps have been linked in some way to the inauguration of these ancient kings? The Moot (Meeting) Hill at Scone, in the eleventh century, was known as Scone 'of the High Shields' and 'of the Melodious Shields', referring surely to the clash of warriors' shields acclaiming their new king.

Sadly, no regalia have survived from early medieval Scotland. Our earliest representation of a Scottish king bearing his symbols of sovereign power comes in the reign of King Edgar (1097–1107). On a royal seal Edgar is depicted wearing a crown and carrying a sceptre and sword, whilst a seal of his successor, King Alexander I (1107–24), depicts him holding an orb. In a miniature painting from a charter to Kelso Abbey, dated 1159, Alexander's successor, King David I (1124–53) and David's successor, his grandson King Malcolm IV (1153–65), are both shown wearing crowns, with David holding a sword and orb and Malcolm a sword and sceptre. There is record of an orb being stolen by Edward I of England (together with the Stone of Destiny and other Scottish

regalia) in 1296 and deposited in Westminster Abbey.

By the thirteenth century the Scottish kings were attaching far greater importance to the Christian rites of coronation and anointment practised on the Continent and were determined to give them a central place in the 'kingmaking' ceremony. This was a perfectly understandable concern. A king not dignified by these Christian emblems and rites at his enthronement was not considered fully a sovereign king.

King Alexander II (1214–49) made several appeals to the Pope for the privilege of Kings of Scots to be crowned and anointed. All were rejected following representations by the English king Henry III, who was determined to limit the authority of the Kings of Scots. An important breakthrough came in 1251, two years after the inauguration of Alexander III (1249–86) at Scone, when Pope Innocent IV finally refused King Henry's submission that English agreement had to be obtained before Kings of Scots could be anointed and crowned. It was to be a further 78 years, however, before full papal recognition would be granted.

The first written record of the Crown and other Royal Regalia occurs at the close of the short and ill-starred reign of John Balliol (1292–96). In a little under four years this luckless monarch, placed on the throne as a vassal of the English King Edward I, had lost his crown and all the trappings of kingship. His reign came to an end in 1296 in a humiliating ceremony held at Montrose Castle before the English king. The chronicler, Andrew of Wyntoun, described the spectacle:

Carved footprint at the fortress of Dunadd, possibly part of an ancient inauguration ceremony.

This Iohun the Balliol dispoyilzeide he
Off al his robis of ryalte.
The pellour thai tuk out of his tabart,
Twme Tabart he was callit eftirwart;
And al vthire insignyis
That fel to kynge on ony wise,
Baythe septure, suerde, crowne and rynge,
Fra this Iohun, that he made kynge,
Hallely fra hym he tuk thare
And mad hym of his kynrik bare.

This John of Balliol deprived he
Of all his robes of royalty.
The fur they took out of his coat,
Empty Coat he was called afterwards;
And all other insignia
That fell to king in any way,
Both sceptre, sword, crown and ring,
From this John, that he made king,
Wholly from him he took there,
And made him of his kingdom bare.

The Sceptre, Sword, Crown and Ring removed that day from King John did not stay long in Scotland. They were taken almost immediately to England along with the other treasures looted from the royal castles. One other powerful symbol of Scottish

John Balliol's crown and sceptre and broken and his tabard in tatters in this sixteenth-century illustration, reflecting his loss of the Scottish kingship in 1296.

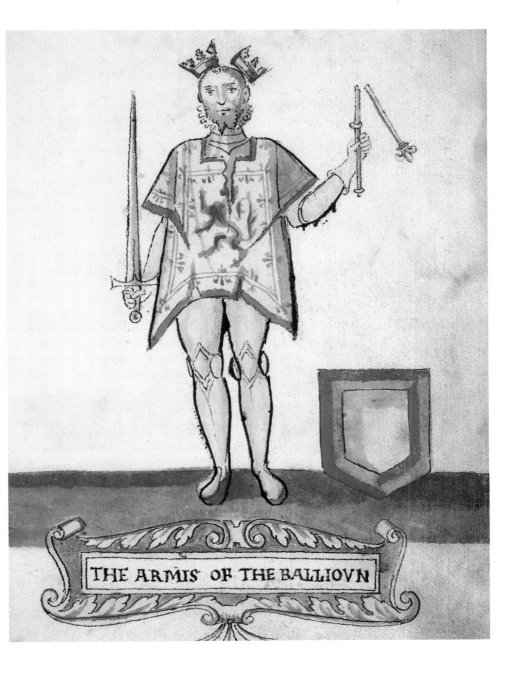

THE ARMIS OF THE BALLIOVN

kingship – the Stone of Destiny, or Stone of Scone, on which the kings were set at their enthronement – was also taken south to England with the Regalia.

THE CORONATION OF KING ROBERT THE BRUCE

When Robert the Bruce seized the throne of Scotland in 1306, both the Stone of Destiny and the Honours were well beyond his grasp. But new symbols of sovereignty could be easily fashioned. Bruce duly journeyed to the ancient Moot Hill of Scone in the spring of that year, to be set upon his throne on Lady Day, Friday 25 March. A hastily made circlet of gold was placed upon the King's head. In his historical epic *The Bruce*, written around 70 years after this inauguration, poet John Barbour wrote:

> *And then in haste to Scone rode he,*
> *And there was crowned without delay*
> *All in the manner of that day*
> *And on the royal throne was set.*

Two days later, on Palm Sunday, the newly crowned king attended a High Mass in the abbey church there. As Christ had entered Jerusalem, so King Robert now entered his kingdom.

No sooner had he done so than he was forced to leave it. Within three months of the ceremony at Scone, his army was routed in battle near Methven, a short distance away, and Bruce fled west to escape the wrath of King Edward of England. Such

Robert the Bruce was one of the many kings crowned at Scone's Moot Hill – recreated here for the Honours exhibition in Edinburgh Castle.

Robt de Frekyn Willam de ...

Robt Seneschaft Garden ...

was the confusion that the newly made golden circlet fell into English hands once more and it was taken south to England. There is no record that it was ever returned and the legend that Bruce's circlet of gold forms part of the present Crown may well be false.

King Robert I (1306–29) must surely have commanded that new Honours be made following his thunderous victory over the English at Bannockburn in June 1314: such was the importance he attached to 'the honours which go with the rule of the realm of Scotland'. Fifteen years later, as the elderly king lay dying at his manor at Cardross, beside royal Dumbarton Castle on the northern shore of the Firth of Clyde, his ambassador, Master Alexander Kinninmonth, at last won the consent of the Pope to the crowning and anointing of the Scottish kings. The papal bull, issued just six days after King Robert had died, was final recognition by Christendom's highest authority of the independence of the Scottish kingdom. The crowning, which for so long had played a secondary part in the inauguration of her kings, was now pre-eminent.

With King Robert dead, the Scots soon exercised their right of crowning and anointing a new king. Bruce's only son, David II (1329–71), at the tender age of five, was duly enthroned at Scone on 24 November 1331. By all accounts it was a ceremony of great and solemn splendour, with no expense spared. A special Sceptre was made to fit the young king's hands. According to John of

King David II of Scotland (left) and Edward III of England in a detail from a fourteenth-century manuscript, agreeing a treaty amidst ongoing tension between the two countries.

Fordun, the chronicler, David was:

> ... anointed King of Scotland, and crowned, by
> the Lord James Bennet, Bishop of St Andrews,
> specially appointed thereunto by a Bull of the most
> holy father John XXII. We do not read that any
> of the Kings of Scotland, before this David, were
> anointed, or with such solemnity crowned.

The coronation of King David II confirmed Scotland's status as a truly independent nation, her sovereign answerable to no one but the Holy Father. The Crown, Sceptre and Sword of State received by the King on that November day were the visible manifestation of that independence.

It is assumed that these same symbols of sovereign power were presented to King David II's successor, his nephew King Robert II (1371–90), the first sovereign of the Royal House of Stewart, and to his successors until the reign of King James IV, who ascended the throne in 1488. But what became of these ancient Regalia, last used at King James IV's coronation, remains a mystery. During King James's reign and that of his son, King James V, they were replaced by the Honours that are now displayed in Edinburgh Castle's Crown Room.

CHAPTER 2
THE CREATION OF
THE HONOURS

KING JAMES IV AND THE PAPAL GIFTS

The slim Sceptre with its elaborate finial (ornamental top) and the awesome Sword of State were created in the warm climes of Renaissance Italy by craftsmen working for the Supreme Pontiff of the Christian world – the Pope in Rome. Papal support had been vital to the sovereigns of Scotland in the prolonged Wars of Independence when England had sought to dominate its poorer northern neighbour. One result of pontifical support was the status of Scotland as a 'special daughter' of the Holy See.

The exchange of gifts was an important and integral part of political life in the Middle Ages. Any papal gift to a European monarch had immense prestige and religious significance. One such gift was the Golden Rose. This was in the form of a cluster of roses mounted on a stem attached to a pedestal base. Flowers and leaves were of pure gold. The largest flower was set with a precious stone of reddish hue, such as an amethyst, and also had a receptacle for balsam and musk to give fragrance to the rose. The Golden Rose conveyed a spiritual message and was a symbol of papal esteem for the recipient.

Portrait of Pope Julius II, the 'Warrior Pope' who gifted the Sword of State to James IV in 1507.

On 5 March 1486 Pope Innocent VIII announced that James III King of Scots (1460–88) would be presented with the Golden Rose. This was a singular honour to the sovereign of a small realm beyond the mainland of Europe. The last papal gift to Scotland had been made three centuries before, in 1182 when King William the Lion (1165–1214) received the Golden Rose from Pope Lucius II. During May 1486, the papal legate Giacomo Passarella, Bishop of Imola, delivered the Rose itself to King James. It was to be the first of a remarkable series of gifts from the popes.

King James III was succeeded by his son James IV. Despite the part played by the latter in the downfall of his father, it did not alter the benevolence of Pope Innocent VIII who repeated the gift of a Golden Rose to the new King of Scots in 1491. Unfortunately, neither of the Roses withstood the vagaries of Scottish history.

It is possible that the silver-gilt Sceptre, the earliest of the Scottish papal gifts to survive, was presented to King James IV at the same time as the Golden Rose. But tradition has it that the Sceptre was a gift in 1494 from Pope Alexander VI, who succeeded Innocent VIII.

In 1502, to complement the Sceptre, King James IV ordered a Sword of Honour, with a scabbard, from the Edinburgh cutler Robert Selkirk. This was carried by the crowned King, also holding his papal Sceptre, the following year at a meeting of the Parliament. However, the native-made Sword was soon superseded by yet another munificent papal gift to the King, this time from Pope Julius II. He was the 'Warrior Pope', who commissioned the artist Michelangelo to paint the ceiling of the Sistine Chapel

Head of the Sceptre with its crystal globe. This is the oldest of the surviving Scottish papal gifts.

in Rome. The Pope actually presented two gifts: a Blessed Sword and a Consecrated Hat. These were formally handed to the King during a solemn High Mass on Easter Sunday 1507 in the Gothic splendour of the abbey church of Holyrood. The papal envoy was an Italian knight named Antonio Inviziati. He had set out from Italy in December 1506 accompanied by his retinue and arrived in Scotland on 31 March 1507. King James was very conscious of the honour accorded him and sent a fulsome letter of gratitude to the Pope.

The Sword and Scabbard were made by Domenico da Sutri. They were created in the period of the High Renaissance and their sumptuous appearance reflects the decorative style then in vogue in Italy. Da Sutri took the Arms of Pope Julius as the theme for the decoration of the Sword handle, scabbard and belt. The oak tree and acorns, symbols of the Risen Christ, plus the dolphins, symbolic of Christ's Church, form part of an imaginative and meaningful ornamentation whose quality exceeds that on the Crown and Sceptre.

Two other swords made by da Sutri as papal gifts have also survived. They are very similar in appearance to the Scottish Sword of State. One was presented to King Ladislaus II of Hungary in 1509 and, because it is in a better state of preservation, indicates what has been lost from the Scottish Sword. The buckle holes on the belt, for example, are reinforced by small silver-gilt sprays of oak leaves and acorns. The second sword, a gift to the Swiss Cantons in 1511, has lost part of one dolphin quillon. Both scabbards are undamaged.

An ornate oak and acorns decoration on the scabbard.

The Consecrated Hat presented to King James IV with the Sword has not survived. Extant examples from the sixteenth century are made of dark crimson velvet, lined with ermine. They have a stiff high crown surrounded by a deep brim which curves upwards to a point at the front. There are two lappets (ornamental ribbons) hanging down from the back. On the right-hand side of the Hat an embroidered gold dove, decorated with pearls, symbolises the Holy Spirit. From the top of the crown alternate straight and wavy rays, outlined in gold thread and filled with seed pearls, descend towards the brim.

THE SWORD OF STATE

The steel blade of the Sword is just under a metre long and 4.4cm wide at its broadest part. Near the cross guard at the top, the blade is etched on each side. One side has the figure of St Peter, the other St Paul. Beneath each are etched the words: JULIUS II PONT MAX (Julius II Supreme Pontiff). The etched lines of the figures and lettering were originally inlaid with gold.

The silver-gilt hilt (or handle) for the blade is around 40cm long with dolphin-shaped quillons (the cross guard between the hilt and blade). The hilt was all of repoussé work but at some stage the dolphins have been cast from the originals and replaced, possibly by the goldsmith Matthew Auchinleck in 1516. The grip above the quillons is decorated with oak leaves and acorns and terminates in a circular pommel (ornamented top) which once had inset enamelled plates. At the bottom of the handle are two stylised oak leaves (broken at the points) which overlap the scabbard at its mouth.

Silver-gilt hilt of the Sword of State.

The Sword, scabbard and belt – papal gifts from Julius II in 1507.

The scabbard for the Sword is made of wood, covered in dark red velvet and mounted with silver-gilt repoussé work. On the front of the scabbard at the mouth is an enamelled panel bearing the Arms of Pope Julius II. Above the Arms is the symbol of the papacy – crossed keys linked by a tasselled cord surmounted by the papal tiara. The remaining length of the scabbard is divided into three areas by two circles which once held enamelled plates.

The three areas are filled with elaborate decoration (missing in places) of oak leaves, acorns, dolphins and grotesque masks. This form of ornament is repeated on the reverse of the scabbard though sections are missing. There are fittings for the sword belt on the reverse near the mouth of the scabbard.

The sword belt is 1.5m long. It is of woven silk and gold thread featuring the personal Arms of Pope Julius repeated along the whole length, each shield shape being linked to the next with leafy ornament. The belt is fastened by a massive silver-gilt buckle with hinged prongs.

THE SCEPTRE AND KING JAMES V

King James IV was killed fighting the forces of Henry VIII of England at the Battle of Flodden in 1513. His heir was an infant son and Scotland was governed by a regent until King James V, aged sixteen, finally took power into his own hands in 1528. European politics at the time placed James V in a position where his favours were sought by the Pope, the Emperor, and the kings of France and England. Conscious of his kingly prestige James sought to

The front and back of the decorative Renaissance scabbard, which is over 1m in length.

enhance the symbols of his sovereignty – the Sceptre and the Crown. He began with the Sceptre.

In 1536 the Edinburgh goldsmith Adam Leys remodelled the Sceptre and added to its length. When presented to King James IV, the Sceptre had consisted of a handle attached to a hexagonal rod with a finial incorporating a ball of rock crystal. Leys appears to have taken moulds of the Italian-made finial and cast the work anew in solid silver, adding another section to the hexagonal shaft. The extra length makes the appearance of the Sceptre instantly more impressive.

This, the earliest surviving papal gift, now consists of the original handle attached to a hexagonal rod, engraved on three of its six sides with urns, leaves and grotesque masks. A knop (ornamental knob) divides the original pieces from the new section. This has been engraved with thistles and fleurs de lis with the King's initials (IR5 for Jacobus Rex V) engraved at the top of the rod.

The finial is flanked by stylised dolphins with tails curling round applied flower shapes. Between the dolphins are three small figures, each under a Gothic canopy.

The first figure is the Virgin, crowned with an open crown, holding the naked Child on her right arm. She carries an orb in her left hand. To the left of the Virgin and Child is St James with a book in his right hand and a staff in his left. This has been broken, and the top is missing. Damage has also occurred to the third figure, St Andrew, patron and protector of Scotland. He holds an open book in his left hand; with his right he grasps a

The Sceptre, remodelled during the reign of James V.

saltire cross which has lost the upper two arms.

Above this group is a polished globe of rock crystal, a substance believed in the Middle Ages to have mystical properties. The crystal is kept in place by three silver strips which come together at the top to support a pierced knop. The finial terminates with another small golden globe surmounted by a pearl.

One small, but important, consequence of enhancing the Sceptre was a change in the Royal Arms of Scotland. Part of the Arms is the crest, which is located on top of the helmet above the shield. From about 1502, the Scottish crest consisted of a seated crowned lion holding a sword in one paw and a flag in the other. At the time the Sceptre was lengthened, the saltire flag on the crest was replaced with a sceptre. This change allows the crest lion to hold two of the Honours of Scotland – the Sword and Sceptre – and to wear the third, the Crown. Thus representations of the Regalia became part of the Royal Arms of Scotland.

THE CROWN OF SCOTLAND AND KING JAMES V

At the end of 1536, King James V sailed to the Continent where he married Princess Madeleine, daughter of Francis I, King of France. The marriage took place on 1 January 1537 in the Cathedral of Notre-Dame in Paris. The royal couple remained in France until May. While residing at Compiègne on 19 February, James was presented with a Blessed Sword and Consecrated Hat from the papal legate acting for Pope Paul III. Although these additional examples of papal favour were carried back to Scotland, neither has survived.

Finial on the Sceptre showing St Andrew reading.

Sadly, Madeleine died within seven weeks of her arrival in Scotland and before she could be crowned Queen. James soon found a new French bride and married Mary of Guise in 1538. The coronation of Queen Mary in February 1540 provided the King with the opportunity to consider the condition of his own crown.

We can only speculate on the shape of the crown inherited by King James V. From the reign of King Edgar (1097–1107) to the reign of King James II (1437–60) the Crown of Scotland is shown as a circular fillet with a varying number of fleurs de lis round the rim, as depicted, for example, on the Trinity Altarpiece, showing King James III at prayer, painted in Bruges in c1471.

The first evidence for a change of shape appears on a silver coin struck in 1484, late in the reign of King James III. The coin is a groat bearing a portrait of the monarch wearing his crown. The royal Crown consists of a band with eight fleurs de lis and four arches surmounted by an orb and cross. This form of crown is described as 'imperial', or 'closed'. Several monarchs of ancient independent European kingdoms adopted the arched crown towards the end of the fifteenth century.

The earliest illustration of King James IV wearing an imperial crown is in the *Book of Hours* made for him to commemorate his marriage to Margaret Tudor, daughter of King Henry VII of England in 1503. The Crown has eight larger fleurs de lis with alternate smaller fleurs de lis or crosses. There are four arches, each decorated with four applied ornaments, surmounted by a

James III of Scotland is crowned by St Andrew, accompanied by his son James. One of the panels of the Trinity Altarpiece by Hugo Van der Goes, this is thought to have been painted for the Collegiate Church of the Holy Trinity, Edinburgh in 1478.

Double portrait of James V and Mary of Guise – an 1895 copy of the original painting.

small orb and cross. The Crown appears to be set with precious stones and pearls. The general appearance is delicate, suggesting that it does not contain a great mass of gold.

However, it must be questioned whether the depiction of the Crown in the *Book of Hours* is accurate. The artist who painted it lived and worked in Bruges and most probably never saw either King James IV or the Scottish Crown. He would not have taken the King's likeness from a real-life portrait but from generic images on coins and seals.

There is every good reason for thinking that the imperial crown dates not from the reign of King James IV but from that of his son, King James V. In May 1532, according to the *Treasurer's Accounts*, a sizeable quantity of gold was purchased from two goldsmiths, Thomas Wood and James Acheson, to enable Adam Leys to mend the Crown 'and making of the spryngis thairto'; these springs conceivably refer to the arches of the Crown. That same account also records the purchase of a velvet bonnet for the Crown. King James may well have had his impressive new 'imperial' crown made so that he could wear it at the opening of his new College of Justice in Edinburgh later that year, and suitably impress all those gathered there that day.

By the time an inventory of royal jewels was made in March 1539, further damage had been done to the Crown. On this occasion the repair work was entrusted to John Mosman, a member of the Incorporation of Goldsmiths in Edinburgh. Mosman had already

A silver coin minted at Edinburgh in 1484 during the reign of King James III.

been commissioned to make the crown for Queen Mary to wear at her own coronation on 22 February 1540. Now he set about refashioning the Crown of Scotland itself. His craftsmanship is typical of Scottish work at the time, lacking the fine skill shown by the best contemporary Continental goldsmiths.

Apart from receiving the damaged Crown, Mosman was also given from the Mint 41 ounces of gold which had been mined at Crawford Moor in Upper Clydesdale, affectionately known as 'God's treasure-house in Scotland'. Mosman was also sent to France in September 1539 to buy 'certane gold werk' with £50 granted by special precept of the King. This was a substantial sum and may well have been spent on purchasing the enamelled orb and cross that now graces the top of the Crown, as well as the bonnet jewels. He was also paid for 22 precious stones to add to the 20 gemstones and 68 pearls in the broken Crown. Among the new stones were three large garnets and a large amethyst.

With that extra gold, new stones and finial Mosman set about remodelling the Crown. Both the sequence of construction and the new work undertaken by him can be deduced from the Crown itself.

John Mosman started by dismantling the four arches from the broken Crown, then carefully removing the existing stones and pearls. He melted down the remaining circlet and added the extra 41 ounces of Scottish gold. He then made a broad flat band edged top and bottom with a decorative strip, which he formed into an oval and soldered together to form the basic circlet.

Mosman next attached a curved ring of forty gold half

The Crown of Scotland as crafted by John Mosman and first worn by James V in 1540.

circles to the top edge of the circlet, each half circle separated by a pearl. He then added to it ten alternating gold fleurs de lis and ten gold crosses fleury (crosses adorned with flowers). The crosses fleury are enriched by four pearls surrounding a central transparent gemstone. The twenty precious stones from the old Crown – either circular, square, triangular, or lozenge-shaped – were set below the twenty fleurs de lis and crosses fleury and placed in individual claw settings. These are contained within ovoid rectangular frames with leaf-shaped sides and enamelled top and bottom sections. The frames were individually made and attached to the circlet. Between the enamelled settings are 22 large oriental pearls. The circlet and its decoration are all new work by John Mosman.

To the circlet Mosman added the four arches from the old Crown, each decorated with three gold and red-enamelled oak leaves (two are replacements). At the point where the arches meet there is an ornament of four chased gold leaves, which are the base for the orb and cross. The orb is made of gold, enamelled blue and spangled with small stars which have been left uncoloured. Horizontal and vertical bands enclose the upper part of the orb and at one time four jewels hung from the horizontal band. Above the orb is a gold cross with leafy ornament on the arms, set off with black enamel. In the centre of the cross at the front is the large amethyst. At the foot of the cross on the back is a small rectangular panel with the letters IR5 for Jacobus Rex V. The cross is enhanced with eight oriental pearls held in place with small gold rosettes.

The Crown with the red velvet bonnet fashioned in 1993.

To complete the Crown, King James ordered a purple velvet bonnet lined with purple satin. The old Crown had a bonnet from at least 1503 which was renewed in 1532. The new bonnet was tailored by Thomas Arthur of Edinburgh who charged 5 shillings for manufacture and £3 12s 6d for the materials. Mosman drilled four pairs of small holes on the lower moulding of the circlet to enable the bonnet to be stitched to the Crown. (The bonnet has been replaced on several occasions. King James VII ordered that the colour of the bonnet be changed to red. The present bonnet was made in 1993.)

The final touch of richness is given by four delicate ornaments, adorned with an oriental pearl set on a pierced oblong of gold, all enamelled in red, blue, green and white. These are attached to the bonnet between the four arches.

When the refashioned Crown of Scotland was complete it weighed 1.6kg (3lb 10oz) and Mosman arranged for John Paterson to make a box to hold it. On 13 February 1540 the new Crown was delivered to the King at the Palace of Holyroodhouse, by now the favoured residence of the royal family in Edinburgh. King James wore it for the first time at his consort's coronation nine days later, in the abbey church of Holyrood. His Majesty was clearly keen to exploit the political symbolism attached to a 'closed' or 'imperial' crown rather than an 'open' crown or circlet, for as Andrea Thomas points out in her biography of James V, *Princelie Majestie*, it 'stressed his status as a sovereign prince, acknowledging no superior authority before God'.

Topping the Crown are an enamelled orb and gold cross, most probably of French origin.

CHAPTER 3
THE AUTHORITY OF THE HONOURS

THE CORONATION OF MARY QUEEN OF SCOTS

King James V died on 14 December 1542 at Falkland Palace, in Fife, at the early age of 30. Just six days earlier his second queen, Mary of Guise, had given birth to a baby girl in the royal palace at Linlithgow. She was named Mary after her mother.

Scotland was then at war with England and, for the child's safety, she was moved to the secure refuge of Stirling Castle. On Sunday 9 September 1543, the nine-month-old infant was wrapped in the Royal Robes and carried in solemn procession from the Palace across the courtyard and into the Chapel Royal. There she was crowned Queen of Scots. The Honours were taken from Edinburgh Castle for the occasion and the new Crown was used for the first time at the coronation of a sovereign of Scotland. Indeed, the three Honours we see today – Crown, Sceptre and Sword of State – were first used together at Mary's crowning.

It must surely have been the most moving of occasions in view of Mary's young age. As Governor of Scotland, the Earl of Arran bore the Crown; the Earl of Lennox, later to be Mary's father-in-law, bore the Sceptre. Cardinal Beaton consecrated the little queen, placing the Crown upon her infant brow, the Sceptre in

An eighteenth-century engraving of Stirling Castle, where the Coronation of Mary Queen of Scots took place.

her tiny hand and girding her with the mighty Sword of State. Like many a child at its christening, Mary cried throughout the entire ceremony!

QUEEN MARY AND PRINCE JAMES

At the age of five, Mary was sent to France for safety. There she married the Dauphin, became Queen of France and was widowed – all by the time she was eighteen. While in France Mary received the Golden Rose from Pope Pius IV in 1560, the fourth Scottish monarch to be so honoured.

In the following year Mary returned to Scotland and, in 1565, married Henry, Lord Darnley. She bore him a son, James, on 19 June 1566, in a small room within the Palace in Edinburgh Castle. The baby was taken from his mother's arms straightaway and carried to Stirling Castle. Within a year of the Prince's birth, his father Darnley had been murdered and his mother Mary had remarried and been forced to abdicate in favour of her son. In May 1568 she fled the country never to return. In her Letters of Abdication, Queen Mary wrote:

> *nothing earthly can be more comfortable and*
> *happy to Us in this earth, than in Our lifetime to*
> *see Our most dear son, the native Prince of this*
> *Our Realm placed in the Kingdom thereof, and the*
> *Crown Royal set upon his head.*

Mary, Queen of Scots, painted around 1560, when she would have been in her late teens. She would leave France the following year to resume her personal reign as Queen of Scots.

For the third time in a century the new monarch of Scotland was an infant. King James VI was crowned at Stirling on 29 July 1567, in the Kirk of the Holy Rude. The Crown, Sceptre and Sword brought from Edinburgh Castle for the occasion, were placed briefly upon the thirteen-month-old child and returned to Edinburgh immediately afterwards.

THE HONOURS AND THE 'LANG SIEGE'

The Keeper of Edinburgh Castle who had authorised the despatch of the Honours to Stirling was James Balfour of Pittendreich. Not long after, he was replaced as Keeper by Sir William Kirkcaldy of Grange, who was charged by the Regent, the Earl of Moray (the deposed Queen's half-brother), to maintain the 'principal strength of the Realm' where 'the king's jewels, moveables, munitionis and registris are kepit' on behalf of the infant king. Mary still had some supporters fighting on her behalf and by 1571 Sir William Kirkcaldy had become one of them, possibly because his patron, the Regent, had been assassinated not long before. Kirkcaldy now steadfastly held the Castle on behalf of his exiled queen and resolutely refused to let the Honours be used by the new Regent, the Earl of Lennox, and his supporting group of nobles.

By this time the Crown, Sceptre and Sword had acquired an additional role to that of coronation regalia. They symbolised the royal presence at meetings of the Parliament, adding to the panoply of majesty, particularly when an infant sovereign could not be present. The Honours were laid on a table

The painted ceiling and frieze in the room in Edinburgh
Castle where James VI was born. This decoration dates from
1617, on the occasion of James' return to his birthplace.

before the monarch's place whenever Parliament met. An Act of Parliament became law only when the King, or his commissioners, took up the Sceptre and used it to touch the relevant document.

Because the Honours were not obtainable for a meeting of the Parliament to be held in Stirling during late August 1571, the Regent devised alternatives. On 17 August an Edinburgh goldsmith, Mungo Bradie, was given 1lb (450g) of silver to manufacture a crown of honour and a sceptre. Bradie also received six gold coins and 340g (12ozs) of mercury to gild the pieces. A sword with a silver-gilt hilt was supplied by a cutler.

The substitute honours were transported from Leith by ship across the Forth to Burntisland where two horses were hired to carry them and Mungo Bradie to Stirling in time for the meeting. These substitutes were again used at a meeting of Parliament held in Edinburgh during April 1573.

By now Sir William Kirkcaldy had been holding the Castle for Queen Mary for almost two years. The siege of the Castle had begun in earnest in the summer of 1571 and had continued in a desultory fashion since. Only after a devastating bombardment in May 1573 did the gallant Kirkcaldy surrender and the Castle fall to the King's party. Not for nothing was it called the 'Lang Siege'. While Kirkcaldy was paying for his loyalty to Mary with his life, the substitute honours were probably being melted down, leaving the real Honours to take their place once more in the life of royal Scotland.

SCOTLAND'S 'SECOND KING'

Certainly from the reign of King James VI, and possibly earlier, the Crown of Scotland was used to crown a 'second king'. Records from the end of the fourteenth century show there were two Kings of Scotland. One was the legitimate monarch of the Scots, the other was the Lord Lyon King of Arms, the royal officer who granted coats of arms to deserving persons on behalf of the sovereign. His official title is derived from the main charge on the Royal Arms of Scotland, a rampant lion.

In 1592 King James appointed David Lindsay of the Mount Secundus as his King of Arms. At Stirling Castle on Saturday 27 May, David Lindsay was knighted by the King and the following day in the Chapel Royal he was crowned by his sovereign with the Crown of Scotland and presented with a baton of office. After the ceremony Sir David, wearing the Crown, dined at the same table as the King.

Twenty-nine years later, on Sunday 17 June 1621, Sir David's successor, his son-in-law Sir Jerome Lindsay, was installed as King of Arms during a ceremony held in the Palace of Holyroodhouse. In the King's absence, he was knighted by the Lord High Chancellor of Scotland, the Earl of Dunfermline, who then placed the Crown of Scotland on the head of the new King of Arms.

Subsequent Lord Lyons were installed in much the same fashion until Sir Charles Erskine of Cambo in 1681. By the time he died in 1727, the Honours of Scotland were no longer available for coronation ceremonies.

The KINGS mone

570 Foot highe

The GENERALLS Lodgeings

THE UNION OF THE CROWNS

In 1578 King James VI's minority came to an end. He ruled Scotland for 25 years, until 1603, the year the unmarried Queen Elizabeth I of England died. James was her heir and he wasted no time in travelling to England to claim the rich throne and be crowned King James I of England also.

James's departure had a profound effect on the significance of the Honours, which remained in Scotland. Because the country now had an absent sovereign these symbols of majesty became a substitute. The aura gained by Crown, Sceptre and Sword after 1603 is part of the continuing respect with which they are regarded to this day. Scotland lost a resident king but gained potent alternatives. The Honours came to embody Scotland in a way which other European Crown Jewels do not, except perhaps the Crown of Hungary which is similarly regarded and respected as the life force of nationhood.

One symbol of this respect was the popularity of the Honours as decorative devices. They had appeared on a coin struck in 1602; afterwards they were painted, carved in wood and stone and rendered in plaster. This respect was further demonstrated between 1615 and 1617, during the course of a major remodelling of the Palace in Edinburgh Castle in time for the 'hamecoming' of King James to his ancient kingdom, to mark his fiftieth anniversary as

King of Scots. A room beside the King's private apartment on the first floor was made ready to serve as a permanent repository for the Honours of Scotland. Stone-vaulted above and below, both for better security and as a precaution against fire, this was the very Crown Room in which the Honours are still stored and displayed.

CHAPTER 4

THE SURVIVAL OF THE HONOURS

TROUBLED TIMES

On 27 March 1625 the 'blessed King James' passed away. His reign had been relatively peaceful. 'Here I sit', he wrote, 'and govern Scotland with my pen … which others could not govern by the sword'.

King James's younger son, Charles, Duke of Albany, succeeded to the throne as King Charles I (his eldest son, Henry, having died in 1612). Although born in Scotland, at Dunfermline Palace on 19 November 1600, Charles was brought up in London and was apt at times to treat his fellow countrymen with disdain. Since the Union of the Crowns of Scotland and England in 1603, the very personal kingship of the Kings of Scots had been replaced by an absentee monarchy. The situation called for wisdom and prudence on the part of the king. King James possessed such pragmatism and diplomacy; King Charles did not, with the direst of consequences both for him and for his country. The Honours of Scotland, the paramount symbols of kingly power, were inevitably caught up in the troubled times that followed.

This gory depiction of the beheading of Charles I in 1649 is likely based on eye-witness accounts and engravings from the time. A few days after the execution, the Scottish Parliament proclaimed Charles II king, angering Oliver Cromwell.

THE CORONATION OF KING CHARLES I

Soon after Charles's accession, plans were made for the King's return to his native land for his coronation as King of Scots. Rumours circulated that he was to come in 1626, but he never appeared. In 1628, and again in 1631, costly preparations were put in hand, but still His Majesty did not return. Eventually Charles did return, in June 1633, to great rejoicing and amid the most elaborate celebrations. The central event of the King's visit was his coronation, which took place on 18 June at the Palace of Holyroodhouse in Edinburgh. The ceremony was one of great pomp and solemnity.

The King spent the night before his coronation in Edinburgh Castle, the last monarch to sleep in the principal royal castle of Scotland. On the following morning, suitably robed and accompanied by the Great Chamberlain, the Lord High Constable, the Earl Marischal and a host of others, he made his way on horseback down the Royal Mile to Holyrood. Before him in the procession were carried the Honours of Scotland: the Spurs borne by the Earl of Eglinton, the Sword of State by the Earl of Buchan, the Sceptre by the Earl of Rothes and finally the Crown itself borne by the Marquis of Douglas.

The ceremony in the Chapel Royal, the old abbey church beside the Palace that received a major upgrade for the occasion, was both lengthy and solemn. For the first part of the service the Honours lay on a little table covered with green velvet laced

Henry, eldest son of James VI and I, is made Prince of Wales by his father, shown here in a 1610 manuscript. But following Henry's death, the Crowns were instead inherited by Charles I.

and fringed with gold and placed close by the communion table. Following the sermon Archbishop Spottiswoode of St Andrews formally presented Charles to his people and anointed him King. Then the coronation proper began.

Firstly the Great Chamberlain mantled the King with the 'Robe Royall', first worn by his grandfather King James V in 1540 and then by his father King James VI at the coronation of Queen Anna, his mother, in 1590. Then the Sword was girded round the King's waist by the Great Constable, and the Spurs put on his feet by the Earl Marischal. Taking the Crown, the Archbishop placed it upon the King's head. Next the Lord Lyon King of Arms proclaimed the new monarch of Scotland's titles before the senior nobility took the oath of allegiance. Following this the Sword was removed from the King by the Great Chamberlain and placed upon the communion table by the Archbishop, who then placed the Sceptre in the King's right hand and enthroned him. Thereafter the remainder of the nobility and the senior clergy paid homage to their new king. At the end of the ceremony the King returned to his state apartments in the Palace cloaked, crowned and carrying the Sceptre. The cannon in the castle fired salvoes in his honour.

It was 'canons' of a quite different sort which helped contribute to King Charles's eventual downfall. These were the Canons of ecclesiastical law issued in 1636. The King's Scottish subjects greatly resented his tampering with the religious life of the nation. As the Bishop of London wrote at the time, the Canons would 'make more noise than all the cannons in Edinburgh Castle'. He was proved right. When in 1637 King Charles foisted on the Scots his Anglican *Book of Common Prayer*, in an attempt to bring the Scots into line with worship in England, they rose up in revolt against him and signed the National Covenant of protest.

With Edinburgh in the grip of Covenanting fever, the Honours were taken secretly from the Castle and removed to Dalkeith Castle for safekeeping. There they remained until April 1639, when the garrison was forced to surrender to the Covenanters. The 'royall ornamentis' were returned to Edinburgh Castle, also by now held by the Covenanters. The King was powerless to intervene. Having got as far as Berwick-upon-Tweed at the head of a reluctant English force, he was prevented from entering Scotland by General Leslie's Covenanting army encamped on Duns Law.

The consequences of this first 'Bishops' War' were momentous not only for the Kingdom of Scotland but also for Charles's other two kingdoms. In 1641 Ireland was in revolt and by August 1642 England too. The consequences for the King himself proved fatal. After surrendering to the Scots in May 1646, he was handed over to the English on 30 January 1647. Exactly two years later, the King was beheaded on the orders of the English House of Commons. Oliver Cromwell now became Lord Protector of the English Commonwealth.

THE CORONATION OF KING CHARLES II
The beheading of King Charles I came as a great shock to the Scots. They may have profoundly disagreed with their king, but

they had no desire to sweep away the monarchy. Within a few days of the King's execution, the Scottish Parliament had proclaimed his son, Charles II, King of Scotland. In June the following year King Charles entered his northern kingdom.

Cromwell, outraged, invaded Scotland. On 3 September 1650 his New Model Army inflicted a humiliating defeat on Leslie's superior forces at Dunbar in East Lothian and threatened to advance on Edinburgh. The King, who had yet to be crowned, as well as the Honours of Scotland, were in grave danger.

Straightaway the Honours were removed from Edinburgh Castle and taken north, probably to the safety of Stirling Castle. At the same time preparations were made for the Coronation of the new King. On 1 January 1651, in the tiny church atop the Moot Hill at Scone, King Charles II was enthroned. It proved to be the last coronation to take place in Scotland.

Despite the great haste, the ceremony was conducted with due pomp and solemnity. Though not so grand as that for his father, it was clearly just as lengthy. 'The exhortatioun wes sumthing large', the chronicler wryly noted, a reference to the overlong sermon delivered by a leading Presbyterian minister. And just as before, the Honours took their place in the proceedings.

Curiously, one feature of his father's coronation at Holyrood was omitted, and another added. King Charles II was not anointed, because it was regarded as a Popish ritual. The 'new' feature was a return to a practice dating from earlier inaugurations of Kings of Scots. The enthronement ceremony ended with the reading of the King's genealogy back to the legendary Fergus I.

CROMWELL AND THE HONOURS

The coronation of King Charles II over, the Honours could not be returned to the security of the Crown Room in Edinburgh Castle, for that fortress had fallen to Cromwell on Christmas Eve 1650. Indeed, the Protector's army was fast advancing on Scone. On 6 June 1651, on the last day of the Parliament held in Perth, the King ordained 'the Erle of Marchell to cause transport the saidis Honouris to the hous of Dunnottor, thair to be keepit by him till farther ordouris'. Dunnottar Castle, sited dramatically on an isolated rocky headland thrusting into the chilly waters of the North Sea, was the ancient stronghold of the Keith family and chief seat of the Earls Marischal of Scotland.

William Keith, sixth Earl Marischal, was at that moment languishing in a prison in the Tower of London, but his representatives carried out the King's instruction and spirited the Honours north-east to Dunnottar. The King meanwhile headed south-west with the Scottish army to England, to defeat at Worcester on 3 September and flight to France. His kingdom and his Honours were at the mercy of Cromwell.

Cromwell was determined to lay his hands on the Scottish Crown Jewels, to do what he had earlier done with those of England – destroy them. His men, under the command of General Monck, took Perth on 2 August but found the cupboard bare. English intelligence suggested that the Honours had gone north-east. Monck followed in hot pursuit. Dundee was taken by storm on 1 September. Aberdonians, probably horrified by the reports coming from Dundee of 1,000 deaths, including 200 women and

An 1886 painting of Cromwell and his forces at Dunbar, where in 1650 he defeated the Scottish army, allowing him to continue his advance through Scotland.

children, opened their gates to Monck's army and escaped with a £1,000 fine. By the end of September, the English were before Dunnottar Castle in strength. Inside the fortress were just 40 men, two sergeants, one lieutenant, their commanding officer, George Ogilvie of Barras, and the Honours of Scotland.

DUNNOTTAR AND DEEDS OF DERRING-DO

The story of how the defenders of Dunnottar withstood the might of Cromwell's army for eight bitter winter months; of how the Honours were smuggled out from the castle under the very noses of the English and hidden beneath the floor of the nearby Kirk of Kinneff; and of how they lay buried there for eight long years until returned once more to Edinburgh Castle, is one of the most well-kent, oft-repeated tales of Scottish history.

No matter that there are greatly conflicting accounts as to how, precisely, the Honours were removed. The most important thing for Scots, then and today, is that the Honours were preserved for posterity. The Lord Chancellor of the day, the Earl of Loudoun, spoke of 'an inexpressible loss and shame if these thingis [meaning the Honours] shall be taken by the enemie'. He spoke for the entire nation. And we today owe a debt to those men and women who gave their lives, or risked doing so, in the preservation of the Honours of Scotland. For without their courage, visitors to the Crown Room in Edinburgh Castle today would not be able to see the oldest set of sovereign regalia in the British Isles.

Oliver Cromwell, Lord Protector of the English Commonwealth, is shown in this c1649 portrait dressed in armour to represent his chivalric qualities and military strength.

One account of the smuggling out of the Honours tells of them being lowered over the walls of the castle on the seaward side, where they were received by a serving woman pretending to gather seaweed. She carried them off, safely concealed in her creel, to the parish kirk at Kinneff, where they were buried beneath the floor.

The more popular, and certainly more thrilling, account has Christian Granger, the minister of Kinneff's wife, and her serving woman as the heroines of the piece. Mrs Granger had obtained leave from the English commander, Colonel Morgan, to enter the castle, on the pretext of visiting the Governor's wife. While there, the Honours were entrusted to her and boldly taken out of the castle, the Crown and Sceptre concealed under her clothes, and the much lengthier Sword and Scabbard in bundles of flax carried by her servant. Legend has it that the breaks visible in both the sword blade and scabbard are a result of the serving woman attempting to make this concealment more effective. Together they passed through the English camp without suspicion. On reaching her horse, Mrs Granger was temporarily thrown into a panic when the Colonel politely assisted her to mount. His suspicions were not aroused and the two women, with the Honours, were safe – for the moment.

The Honours were hidden first, it is said, at the bottom of the bed in the manse until the minister could bury them more securely in the kirk. 'For the Crown and Sceptre', he later wrote to the Countess Marischal, 'I raised the pavement-stone just before the pulpit, in the night tyme, and digged under it ane hole, and

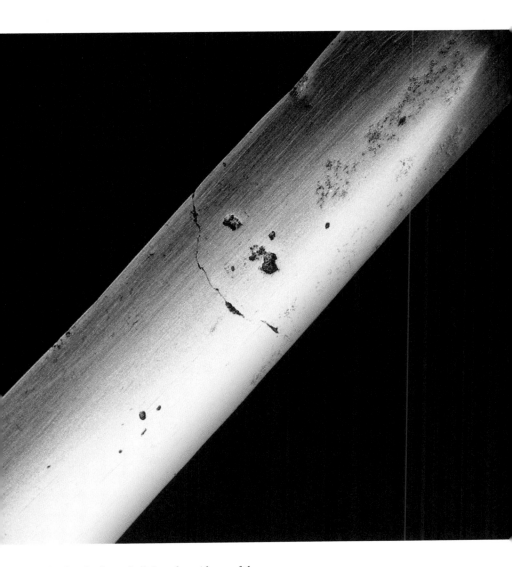

The broken (and mended) Sword – evidence of the
struggles undertaken to protect the Honours.

put them in there, and filled up the hole, and layed down the stone just as it was before, and removed the mould that remained, that none would have discerned the stone to have been raised at all. The Sword again, at the west end of the church, amongst some common saits [pews] that stand there, I digged down in the ground betwixt the twa foremost, and laid it doun without the case [scabbard] of it, and covered it up'.

On 26 May 1652, the long siege of Dunnottar Castle finally ended. It was the last stronghold to fall to the English. Cromwell was clearly still confident that the Scottish Regalia were within his grasp for one of the articles of capitulation of the garrison provided 'that the Croun and Scepter of Scotland, together with all other ensigns of Regallitie, be delivered to mee'. He was to be bitterly disappointed once again. Angry and frustrated, Cromwell's men plundered the castle of its remaining treasures while the governor and his lady were harshly imprisoned. Neither would give up their secret, however, and though George Ogilvie lived to tell the tale, his wife died from the effects of her treatment.

While Cromwell held sway over Scotland, the Honours were never safe. Every now and then, Mr and Mrs Granger went to the kirk at the dead of night to lift the Honours out from their hiding places and make sure that all was well.

Gradually the threat from the English troops billeted nearby faded, possibly because of a growing rumour that the Honours had been smuggled out of the castle, over the sea to France.

The Burying of the Scottish Regalia painted around 1846 is an atmospheric recreation of the Honours being buried in Kinneff Kirk to prevent them from falling into English hands.

Cromwell died in 1658. Two years later, on 14 May 1660, in Edinburgh, King Charles II was proclaimed King of three kingdoms. As the Honours were returned to Edinburgh Castle, the cannon fired in salute. The sovereign was overjoyed, and in a letter dated 4 September of that year His Majesty wrote to the Countess Marischal:

> *Madame I am so sensible of the good service done to me in preserving my Crowne Sceptre & Sword that as I have put marks of my favor on yor sons so I could not let them goe to Scotland without acknowledging also my sense of yor kindness & care in that & in other things relating to my service during my absence. I do desire those things may be deliverd to my Lord Marishall that as he received them so they may be deliverd by him to the ensuing Parliament. And shall only adde that on all occasions you shall find me*
>
> *Your affectionate friend*
> *Charles R*
> *Whitehall the 4 of September 1660*

One item of Regalia was not smuggled out to Kinneff Kirk but was retained by George Ogilvie as a memento – the elaborate Sword Belt. In 1790 it was accidentally discovered built into a garden wall at his house at Barras. It was returned by a descendant of his to its rightful place in the Crown Room in Edinburgh Castle in 1892.

Royal Gratitude

A unique heraldic method of expressing thanks was used by King Charles II following his Restoration to reward two of the men involved in preserving the Honours of Scotland from the hands of Cromwell. Each man was given an augmentation, or addition, to his coat of arms which alluded to the Honours of Scotland and the Royal House of Scotland.

The first was John Keith, son of the Earl Marischal, who was helping to defend Dunnottar against Cromwell. He was granted an augmentation of a red sceptre and sword within a saltire, with an imperial crown set within a border of eight silver thistles. He was also made Knight Marischal of Scotland and created, seventeen years later, Earl of Kintore, Lord Keith of Inverurie and Keith Hall.

George Ogilvie of Barras, whose wife died in prison after the taking of Dunnottar Castle, was granted the addition of a crowned thistle to his coat of arms. This is the Royal Plant Badge of Scotland, first used by King James V and still employed by Her Majesty the Queen in Scotland. Ogilvie of Barras also became a Knight Baronet and as Sir George Ogilvie of Barras his armorial ensigns carried the Arms of Nova Scotia.

These royal marks of gratitude became part of the Arms of Kintore and Ogilvie and have been enjoyed by their descendants ever since.

PREVIOUS PAGE **Nineteenth century engraving of Dunnottar Castle where the Honours were taken for protection. When Cromwell laid siege to the castle, the Honours were smuggled out and buried at Kinneff Kirk.**

THE 'SITTING DOWN' OF PARLIAMENT

After 1651 the Honours were never again used to crown a sovereign. Their principal use was now at sittings of the Parliament in Edinburgh. They served to signify the King's presence now that he chose not to visit his northern kingdom. More than ever before, perhaps, these symbols of sovereignty were treated by the nation with a reverence not witnessed while her monarch reigned in person.

From the first meeting of Parliament after the King's Restoration, which sat in January 1661, to the last of all, which was adjourned in March 1707, the Honours were taken in procession out from the Crown Room in the Castle and down to Parliament House in the Royal Mile. There they lay, centre stage, signifying the sovereign's presence, and at the passing of each Act the sovereign's consent was signified by the touching of the Sceptre upon the parchment.

The carriage of the Honours to Parliament, and their transport back again, was carried out with great ceremony. By the late seventeenth century this ancient ceremony had come to be called the 'Ryding of the Parliament'. It was a most elaborate procession, not unlike that for coronations. The representatives of the Three Estates (the clergy, nobility and burgesses) walked before the senior Officers of State. Immediately behind the Lyon King of Arms came the Crown, Sceptre and Sword, in that order, borne by the appropriate dignitaries and attended by Heralds and other members of the College of Arms. Throughout the progress, trumpets sounded and cannons roared from the battlements of the Castle.

THE UNION OF THE PARLIAMENTS

When Parliament assembled on 3 October 1706 it proved to be for the last time. With the Honours in their accustomed place in Parliament House, the members debated long and hard on the matter in hand – union with England. At last, on 16 January 1707, the Treaty of Union was formally ratified and the Lord Chancellor, the Earl of Seafield, touched the Act with the Sceptre. Handing it back to the clerk, Chancellor Seafield uttered the immortal words: 'Now, there's an end of an auld sang.'

Of the 25 Articles of Union in the Treaty, one referred to the Honours themselves. During the heated debate great concern had been expressed that the Regalia might be carried off to London, never to return. Though many parts of the Treaty were the subject of intense discussion, not a single voice spoke out against the declaration in Article XXIV that:

> *the Croun, Sceptre, and Sword of State …*
> *continue to be kept as they are within that part*
> *of the United Kingdom now called Scotland; and*
> *that they shall so remain in all times coming,*
> *notwithstanding the Union.*

The Treaty of Union, including the Article referring to the Honours of Scotland, was approved by the English Parliament on 19 March. Both Parliaments were now no more; a new United Kingdom Parliament would meet, in London, from now on.

The Scottish Parliament was adjourned on 26 March. The Honours were now deprived of all practical use, either as

coronation insignia or as symbols of sovereignty at sittings of the Parliament. A farewell speech was composed for the Crown:

> *I royal diadem relinquished stand*
> *By all my friends and robbed of my land*
> *So left bereft of all I did command ...*

The Honours were handed over to the Lord Treasurer-Depute and taken back up to the Castle. There, in the stone-vaulted Crown Room which had been built for them 90 years before, they were safely locked away in the great oak chest for another time. The openings into the vault were walled up and the Honours of Scotland, the symbols of sovereignty for more than two hundred years, were left in peace.

The Sceptre and the Articles of Union, the treaty that was signed and sealed by commissioners appointed by Queen Anne. This created a new parliament for the United Kingdom, and also led to the Honours being secreted away in Edinburgh Castle.

CHAPTER 5
THE HONOURS
REDISCOVERED

The Honours lay entombed within the Crown Room in the Castle. In time, people began to question whether they had ever been placed there, and rumours circulated that they had been secretly removed to England in contravention of the Treaty of Union. There was even a report that the ancient Crown of Scotland had been shown in the Tower of London. The closed-up room in the Castle became something of a mystery to the soldiers serving in the garrison.

Eighty-seven years after the Honours had been locked away, on 5 November 1794, the Crown Room was briefly opened up by the Castle's Lieutenant-Governor, Major Drummond, who was searching for some lost Parliamentary records. In the darkened, dust-filled room he saw the great oak chest. He repeatedly shook it, but it returned no sound. With no authority from King George III to open the chest, he left the room and walled up the opening once more, more convinced than ever that the Honours were gone.

WALTER SCOTT DISCOVERS THE HONOURS
The anxiety felt by Major Drummond in 1794 about the fate of the Honours was shared by Walter Scott and the Officers of State

The great oak chest, made in 1617, in which the Honours were locked away following the creation of the United Kingdom in 1707.

with him as, 24 years later, they gathered on the steps outside the Crown Room. They were ready to unblock the doorway once more and this time, armed with the royal warrant, to force open the lid of the great oak chest. As the workmen set to their task, Scott later wrote, 'the general impression that the Regalia had been secretly removed weighed heavily on the hearts of all'.

Their fears were unfounded. As the lid of the chest creaked open, there lay the Crown, Sceptre and Sword precisely as they had been left in 1707. As the glinting Honours of Scotland emerged from their linen wrappings, Walter Scott and those with him in the Crown Room were overwhelmed by uncontrollable joy. The news travelled fast and the people of Scotland were delighted by the rediscovery.

Preparations were now put in hand for the permanent display of the Honours in the Crown Room which had been their home since 1617. A second royal warrant, issued on 8 July 1818, appointed the Keeper of the Great Seal of Scotland, the Keeper of the Privy Seal, His Majesty's Advocate, the Lord Clerk Register and the Lord Justice Clerk to be Commissioners for the Keeping of the Regalia. Their first task was to appoint Sir Adam Ferguson, a friend of Walter Scott, Keeper of the Regalia and to give him a flat in the Palace directly above the Crown Room.

The public were now invited to inspect the Honours for themselves. In 1819 folk were charged the princely sum of one shilling each for the privilege of viewing them. There they have remained ever since.

A nineteenth-century engraving of the Honours in
the Crown room at Edinburgh Castle.

KING GEORGE IV RECEIVES THE HONOURS

In 1821 the Prince Regent, who had granted the royal warrant leading to their rediscovery, was crowned King George IV. The following year he paid the first royal visit to Scotland by a reigning sovereign since that of King Charles II in 1651.

The visit was stage-managed by Walter Scott and on Monday 12 August, shortly before the King's arrival at Leith, the Honours were conveyed in great procession from the Castle by the Knight Marischal, escorted by a troop of Highlanders, to the Palace of Holyroodhouse. They were to remain there for the duration of the King's stay and so 'grace the presence of the King'. The *Edinburgh Evening Courant* reported that 'the pavements of the streets and the windows and balconies, in front of which the procession passed, were crowded with a brilliant association of beauty and fashion.'

Such was the enthusiasm of the Edinburgh public both for the newly discovered Honours and their recently arrived king that among the attractions laid on for the visit was a large representation of an imperial crown, erected on the top of one of the flues at the gasworks, which when illuminated at night 'had a beautiful effect'!

On arriving at the Palace of Holyroodhouse on 15 August, His Majesty formally received the Crown, Sceptre and Sword of State from the Duke of Hamilton, Lord Francis Leveson Gower (representing the Earl of Sutherland) and the Earl of Errol respectively. In touching each emblem, he realised his kingship of the nation.

During a grand ceremony, King George IV is presented with the keys to the Palace of Holyroodhouse and the Honours of Scotland.

In *The Entry of George IV into Edinburgh from the Calton Hill, 1822*, huge crowds are gathered for a rare glimpse of a reigning monarch.

One week later, the King's tour culminated in a grand procession to restore the Honours to the Castle. It was a dreich summer's day but the weather did nothing to dampen the enthusiasm either of the huge crowds that lined the route or of the King himself.

The King 'stood upon the summit of Edina's grey crest', bade the Honours farewell and they were returned to the Crown Room.

The Honours did not leave the Castle again for another 132 years. They did, however, leave the Crown Room.

BURIED ONCE MORE!

The Honours were buried not once but twice in their eventful history. In 1651 they had been concealed from Cromwell; in 1939 they were hidden once more to prevent them from falling into German hands.

At the outbreak of the Second World War the Honours were packed into the great oak chest and taken down to a cellar beneath the Crown Room and covered with sandbags. The worry at that time was the risk of damage from aerial bombardment. But as the war progressed, concern mounted about the likelihood of a German invasion and the possibility of the Honours falling into enemy hands. More serious measures were called for.

On 12 May 1941 the Honours were taken out from the chest, packed into two zinc-lined cases and buried in separate locations in the ruins of David's Tower, the medieval tower house entombed beneath the Half Moon Battery in Edinburgh Castle. The Crown

David's Tower is a medieval tower house built by David II within Edinburgh Castle. It was in these ruins that the Honours were concealed for protection for most of the Second World War.

and the Stewart Jewels were buried beneath the floor of a latrine-closet the Sceptre, Sword of State, Belt, Scabbard and Wand were concealed in a wall. Plans indicating the locations were sealed in envelopes and sent in the utmost secrecy, one each to His Majesty King George VI, the Secretary of State for Scotland, the King's and Lords' Treasurer's Remembrancer and the Governor General of Canada.

When the war ended in victory the Honours were restored once more to public display.

THE NATIONAL SERVICE OF THANKSGIVING, 1953

On Wednesday 24 June 1953, the Honours were taken from the Castle by the Lord Lyon King of Arms and his brother Heralds, escorted by the Queen's Bodyguard for Scotland (the Royal Company of Archers) who marched on each side of an open carriage bearing the Heralds. Lord Lyon held the Crown, Rothesay Herald carried the Sword of State upright and Marchmont Herald cradled the Sceptre on his right arm. All were bareheaded out of respect for the precious burdens in their care.

The destination for the Honours was the High Kirk of St Giles, in Edinburgh's High Street, where a National Service of Thanksgiving took place in the presence of the new sovereign, Queen Elizabeth. The Honours were carried to the Holy Table where they lay throughout the ensuing act of worship. The climax came at the close of the service when the Minister of St Giles presented the Sceptre of Scotland to Her Majesty, who in

The Honours on public display after the end of the Second World War.

turn handed it to the Earl of Crawford and Balcarres. She next received the Sword of State before placing it in the care of the Earl of Home. Finally, the Minister lifted the Crown of Scotland on its cushion from the Holy Table and offered it to the sovereign who took its weight before giving it to the Duke of Hamilton, who was on bended knee. Then, preceded by Her Honours, the Queen and Duke of Edinburgh walked through the congregation to be greeted by the citizens of Edinburgh, who acclaimed the sovereign outside the High Kirk.

THE CROWN OF SCOTLAND AND THE STATE OPENING OF THE SCOTTISH PARLIAMENT

On Thursday 1 July 1999, Her Majesty Queen Elizabeth formally opened the Scottish Parliament, the first to sit for nearly 300 years. Gracing the ceremony was the Crown of Scotland.

On the morning of the opening, the Crown was taken from its resting place in the Crown Room and carried to the Castle's Great Hall. There the royal diadem was formally transferred by the Commissioners for the Keeping of the Regalia into the custody of the Duke of Hamilton, who has the traditional right to bear the Crown of Scotland before the sovereign.

The Scottish Crown, together with the other Honours, had last been taken ceremonially from the Castle for the National Service of Thanksgiving in June 1953. For the opening of the Scottish Parliament the Crown alone was borne in State from the Castle to the ceremony in Edinburgh's Royal Mile. By this time both the Sword of State and the Sceptre were deemed too fragile to move.

THE HONOURS IN THE TWENTY-FIRST CENTURY

The Honours are Scotland's principal royal treasures surviving from the High Middle Ages. Today, over one million people from across the world visit the Crown Room in Edinburgh Castle to view them. They are indeed precious beyond price. Together with the legendary Stone of Destiny, they reflect the history – and mystery – of royal Scotland. However, the Honours are no museum pieces, for they retain an important ceremonial role to this day. The Honours will continue to be presented to new sovereigns at the National Service of Thanksgiving in St Giles' Cathedral, and every four years the Crown of Scotland is taken down to Holyrood to the State Opening of the Scottish Parliament. The Honours and the Stone of Destiny remain an integral part of Scotland's life and culture.

PREVIOUS PAGE Less than a month after her coronation at Westminster Abbey in June 1953, Queen Elizabeth II was presented with the Honours in the National Service of Thanksgiving at St Giles' Cathedral on Edinburgh's Royal Mile.

CHAPTER 6
ADDITIONS TO THE HONOURS

Since 1818, the Honours of Scotland have been joined on display by the following precious royal jewels:

THE WAND

Walter Scott discovered a fourth object in the oak chest alongside the Crown, Sceptre and Sword of State – a one-metre-long silver-gilt wand topped by a globe of rock crystal surmounted by a cross. What its function was, and why it was in the chest at all, have never been satisfactorily answered. It may conceivably have been the baton of office of an official responsible for placing the Honours in the chest following the Treaty of Union with England in 1707, knowing that it would no longer be of service.

THE STEWART JEWELS

These jewels were returned to Scotland in 1830, having passed down through the exiled Stewart family for 119 years. When George III learned of the poverty of Cardinal York, who prior to entering the Catholic Church had been Prince Henry, the last Stewart claimant to the British throne, the King arranged for a handsome annuity to be paid to him. The Cardinal had resisted any temptation to sell the Stewart Jewels, and on his death in 1807

The Lorne Jewels – necklace with locket and pendant.

he left them to King George in thanks. By the express command of King William IV the Jewels were returned to Scotland and deposited in the Crown Room in December 1830.

Undoubtedly the finest of the jewels is the St Andrew Jewel of the Order of the Thistle, the insignia of Scotland's premier Order of Chivalry, founded by King Charles II in 1687. The jewel contains a miniature of Princess Louise of Stolberg, who married Bonnie Prince Charlie in 1772. Two items – the Collar and the Great George – are associated with the Order of the Garter, England's premier Order of Chivalry, and were probably made for King James VII prior to his enforced abdication in 1688. The fourth jewel, a ruby ring encrusted with diamonds, may have been made for King James VI.

THE LORNE JEWELS
A necklace, locket and pendant were bequeathed to the people of Scotland in 1939 by Princess Louise, the fourth daughter of Queen Victoria. She had received the London-made jewels in 1871 as a gift from the Clan Campbell to celebrate her marriage to John Campbell, Marquis of Lorne, later the 9th Duke of Argyll.

THE GREAT OAK CHEST
The Honours of Scotland were stored in the Crown Room in a great iron-bound oak chest. This too survives. It was made in 1617, as part of the works to refashion the Palace in Edinburgh Castle for King James VI's 'hamecoming' to his ancient kingdom, to celebrate his Golden Jubilee as sovereign. The refurbishment

included the provision of a new Crown Room.

The chest had two large iron padlocks and could only be opened when the two Crown representatives tasked with its security appeared together with their separate keys. One of those padlocks survives, and bears testimony to the fact that in 1818 Walter Scott, without the key, had to instruct the King's blacksmith to force it open.

CHAPTER 7

THE STONE OF DESTINY

So if ever ye come on a Stane wi a ring,
Jist sit yersel' doon and proclaim yersel' king;
For there's nane wid be able tae challenge yer claim
That ye'd croon'd yersel' King on the Destiny Stane.
Johnny McEvoy, 'The Wee Magic Stane'

The Stone of Destiny is one of the most powerful icons of Scottish nationhood – the ancient throne on which our monarchs were inaugurated from time immemorial. Today, it rests beside those other symbols of sovereignty, the Honours of Scotland, in the Crown Room at Edinburgh Castle, but it was not always thus, for the Stone of Destiny has had as dramatic a history as the Honours themselves.

FROM LEGEND TO FACT

To our ancestors the Stone of Destiny was Jacob's Pillow, the very rock mentioned in the Book of Genesis on which Jacob rested his head when he dreamt of the ladder rising to Heaven. Another legend tells that the Stone was brought to Argyll, in western Scotland, by the descendants of Scota, daughter of the Pharaoh of Egypt, by way of Spain and Ireland. When King Kenneth mac

The Stone of Destiny, an ancient stone used for the inauguration of Scottish monarchs (and then the coronations of British kings and queens) for hundreds of years.

Alpin combined the kingdoms of the Picts and the Scots in about 843, the Stone was taken to Scone, the ancient Pictish capital near Perth. And there, for the next 450 years, the Kings of Scots were inaugurated by sitting on the Stone at Scone.

Then disaster struck. In 1296 King Edward I of England invaded, forced the abdication of King John Balliol, and ordered that the Stone of Destiny be taken to London and placed in Westminster Abbey. There, for the next 700 years, the monarchs of England, and later of Great Britain, were crowned on the Stone – from King Edward II in 1308 to Queen Elizabeth II in 1953.

On St Andrew's Day (30 November), 1996, by royal warrant, the Stone of Destiny was formally returned to Scotland, and placed in Edinburgh Castle, Scotland's premier royal fortress. It will, however, be taken to Westminster to continue its traditional role in the coronation ceremonies of future sovereigns of the United Kingdom.

The Stone of Destiny is no thing of beauty – indeed, from the outset it was probably never intended to be seen in all its glory but mostly hidden within a wooden chair or throne. Following its return to Scotland in 1996, and prior to its placing in the Crown Room at Edinburgh Castle, the iconic artefact was closely examined by experts in Historic Scotland's Conservation Centre in Edinburgh. They discovered that the Stone itself is formed of a coarse-grained, pinkish-buff sandstone most commonly found in Perthshire and Angus, strongly suggesting that the Stone most probably originated in the neighbourhood of Scone, rather than Argyll or further afield as legend suggests.

PREVIOUS PAGE Jacob rests his head on Jacob's Pillow. One story is that the biblical stone became the Stone of Destiny.

116

The sandstone block measures 67cm x 42cm x 27cm, and at each end is an iron staple carrying an iron figure-of-eight link terminating in a ring. The two rings may have been added to help transport the Stone, most likely when it was moved out of the abbey church at Scone to the graveyard outside, where royal inaugurations took place.

The Stone itself is roughly carved on all surfaces except the top. Its surface reveals evidence for alterations and repairs over the years. Most prominently, on the top is a roughly chiselled rectangular groove, which may well have been intended to hold a cushion for the seated sovereign. These numerous episodes of alteration to the stone, combined with its weathered nature, make it clear that it has been in use for a long period of time. This strengthens the case for the Stone's authenticity. It is simply too complex an artefact to have been produced in haste – whether in 1296 or 1951 – as the conspiracy theorists would have us believe.

INAUGURATION STONE

Though it is assumed that every King of Scots after Kenneth mac Alpin was inaugurated at Scone on the Stone of Destiny, the first to be recorded actually doing so was Lulach, King Macbeth's stepson, who was enthroned on 'the royal seat' in August 1057. Thereafter, the Stone becomes a constant, and pivotal, feature of the inauguration ceremony. The first definite reference to the Stone is in an inventory from 1297. However, detailed information as to how it was used is unrecorded until the inauguration of King Alexander III in July 1249.

John of Fordun, in his *Chronicles of the Scottish People*, details the events of that summer's day when eight-year-old Alexander was enthroned at Scone:

> A great many nobles led Alexander up to the cross which stands in the graveyard, at the east end of the church. There they set him on the royal throne, which was decked with silken cloths inwoven with gold; and the Bishop of St Andrews consecrated him King. So the King sat down upon the royal throne – that is, the stone – while the earls and other nobles, on bended knee, strewed their garments under his feet before the stone.
>
> Now this stone is reverently kept in that monastery, for the consecration of the Kings of Alba [the ancient name for Scotland]; and no King was ever wont to reign in Scotland, unless he had first, on receiving the name of King, sat upon this stone of Scone.
>
> But lo! when all was over, a Highland Scot suddenly fell on his knee before the throne and, bowing his head, hailed the King in his mother tongue [that is, Gaelic] and recited, even unto the end, the pedigree of the Kings of Scots.

The ceremony, secular in origin, was closer to the inauguration of a pagan chieftain than to a coronation. It was held in the open air, and the central act was the setting of the King on a stone, symbolic of his union with the land and its people. The next inauguration was different, more Christian in character and held inside a church. It was also the last occasion a King of Scots was enthroned on the Stone of Destiny.

On St Andrew's Day 1292 John Balliol was 'placed on the regal stone [and] was solemnly crowned in the church of the canons regular at Scone'. William Rishanger, in his *Chronicles and Annals*, makes no mention of an open-air ceremony but describes instead an enthronement more in tune with those elsewhere in Christian Europe at that time.

TROPHY OF WAR

King John Balliol's reign proved short but far from sweet. He was in effect the 'puppet king' for King Edward I of England, who saw himself as 'overlord' of Scotland; fresh from his victory over the Welsh, Edward now believed he could control Scotland also. Poor John Balliol tried in vain to resist. The crucial act of defiance came when Edward, facing war with France, ordered Balliol, together with his earls and barons, to fight in his cause. The Scots refused and instead made a treaty with the French, part of the the famous 'Auld Alliance'. It was the last straw as far as Edward was concerned.

On 28 March 1296 Edward invaded. Crossing the River Tweed at Coldstream, he sacked Berwick, then Scotland's chief town and port (now in England), and defeated the Scottish army at Dunbar. Scotland lay at his mercy. Before July was out he had dethroned

King John Balliol, stripped him of his power, and sent him south to the Tower of London. By the end of August, the royal regalia, records, jewellery, plate and relics, including the Scots' fragment of the True Cross, known as the Black Rood (cross) of St Margaret, had been despatched to the Palace of Westminster. By the end of September, the Stone of Destiny had joined them on the long journey south. Edward's subjects rejoiced:

> *Their kings' seat of Scone*
> *Is driven over down,*
> *To London led.*

Edward wasted no time in showing off his greatest trophy of war – greater even than the Crown of Arthur earlier stolen from the Welsh – which clearly demonstrated his attempts to destroy and remove features of Scottish nationhood and national identity He ordered Walter of Durham to make a gilded wooden throne, the present Coronation Chair, for the Stone to be placed in and had them installed in the Chapel of St Edward the Confessor in Westminster Abbey.

> *I'll tell you truly what the Stone of Scotland is …*
> *Now Edward King of England has taken it,*
> *By the grace of Jesus and by hard fighting.*
> *To Saint Edward has he given it.*

The Stone of Destiny in its Coronation Chair was first used to enthrone an English monarch on 25 February 1308, at the coronation of Edward I's son, King Edward II. Henceforth, all English

The Stone of Destiny in the Coronation Chair, Westminster
Abbey, prior to its removal to Edinburgh Castle in 1996.

monarchs (save Edward V, who was deposed within three months of succeeding to the throne and murdered in the Tower of London) would be crowned seated on Scotland's Stone of Destiny. In the immediate aftermath of the Stone's theft, it does not appear to have been a priority for the Scots to have it returned to its rightful place, even after the bloody Wars of Independence had ended in 1328. They were more concerned at the loss of the Black Rood of St Margaret, which was duly restored. So the Stone of Destiny remained in the Coronation Chair at Westminster Abbey.

Three centuries later, however, something most unexpected occurred – a Scot became King of England. The death in 1603 of Queen Elizabeth I, 'the Virgin Queen', left her nearest surviving relative, King James VI of Scotland, as her successor. He was duly crowned King James I of England on 25 July that year. For many Scots, King James's enthronement on the Stone of Destiny was an ancient prophecy come true:

> *If destiny deceives not, the Scots will reign, 'tis said,*
> *In that same place where the Stone has been laid.*

Sir Walter Scott, in his inimitable fashion, later rendered the prophesy so:

> *Unless the Fates are faithless found,*
> *And prophets' voice be vain,*
> *Where'er this monument is found*
> *The Scottish race shall reign.*

From that time on all but one English monarch, and after the

Treaty of Union of 1707 all but one sovereign of the United Kingdom of Great Britain, have been enthroned on the Stone of Destiny. The exceptions were Queen Mary II in 1689, who was jointly enthroned with her husband, King William III, and perforce sat on a second chair especially made for the occasion, and King Edward VIII, who in 1936 abdicated before his coronation could take place.

RETURN OF THE STONE

For more than 600 years the Stone of Destiny lay in Westminster Abbey. Then, quite out of the blue, in 1924 David Kirkwood, Labour MP for Dumbarton Burghs, and a political activist known for his involvement in the Red Clydeside movement, tabled a bill in the House of Commons for its return; on 15 July the bill passed its first reading by a margin of 30 votes. Among those who voted against was a fellow Scot, Ramsay MacDonald, the Prime Minister. He declined to support further progress of the Bill on the grounds that his government had other legislative priorities. There the matter rested – for the moment.

Where David Kirkwood failed, four Scottish students succeeded. On Christmas Day 1950 Ian Hamilton, Kay Matheson, Alan Stuart and Gavin Vernon contrived, against all the odds, to remove the Stone of Destiny from the Coronation Chair and smuggle it out of Westminster Abbey. They even managed to bring it home to Scotland, despite a huge police hunt. Three months later, on 11 April 1951, the Stone was found lying at the entrance to Arbroath Abbey, where the famous *Declaration of*

Arbroath had been drafted and sealed in 1320. Within 24 hours of its discovery the Stone was on its way back to Westminster. But those four students had succeeded in reigniting the debate as to the Stone of Destiny's permanent location, and the matter quickly returned to the Houses of Parliament. Three options were placed before MPs and Peers – to leave it in Westminster Abbey, to return it to Scotland for custody between coronations, or to arrange for it to be displayed in the capital cities of the Commonwealth, beginning with Edinburgh. Only on 26 February 1952, after lengthy debate within and beyond the Houses of Parliament, did Sir Winston Churchill, the Prime Minister, announce:

> *For over 650 years the Stone has been in*
> *Westminster Abbey and, from its use at successive*
> *Coronations it has a historic significance for*
> *all countries of the Commonwealth. With the*
> *approval of Her Majesty's Government, the Stone*
> *has been restored to its traditional place [that is,*
> *the Coronation Chair in Westminster Abbey].*

It was a close-run thing. Just days earlier King George VI had passed away and a new sovereign, his daughter, now reigned. Her Majesty Queen Elizabeth was enthroned on the Stone of Destiny a little over a year later, on 2 June 1953.

Then, 40 years later, amidst broader political discussions around Scottish devolution, the Stone unexpectedly came to the

The Stone of Destiny being removed from Arbroath
Abbey to a police cell in Forfar, where it was housed
before its return to Westminster Abbey.

forefront once again. On 3 July 1996 – exactly seven centuries after the Stone of Destiny had been stolen – Prime Minister John Major rose to his feet in the House of Commons to declare:

The Stone of Destiny is the most ancient symbol of Scottish kingship. It was used in the Coronation of Scottish Kings until the end of the 13th century. Exactly 700 years ago, in 1296, King Edward I brought it from Scotland and housed it in Westminster Abbey. The Stone remains the property of the Crown. I wish to inform the House that, on the advice of Her Majesty's Ministers, the Queen had agreed that the Stone should be returned to Scotland. The Stone will, of course, be taken to Westminster Abbey to play its traditional role in the Coronation ceremony of future sovereigns of the United Kingdom.

Following this surprise announcement, a consultation process was launched as to where in Scotland the Stone of Destiny might be located. Various sites were proposed that had some association with the Stone, including Scone itself, Stirling Castle and Arbroath Abbey. But it was Edinburgh Castle, and specifically the Crown Room, that emerged as the location most favoured by those responding to the consultation. Arrangements were put in hand immediately for its return, with the expectation that the Stone would be available for public display on St Andrew's

Day. On the morning of 15 November 1996, the Stone of Destiny crossed over the River Tweed at Coldstream, where Edward I's invasion force had crossed in 1296, and was officially welcomed back to Scotland. On the morning of 30 November, it was taken in procession from the Palace of Holyroodhouse up Edinburgh's Royal Mile and, following a service in St Giles' Cathedral, to its new resting place in Edinburgh Castle, where it is still seen by visitors today.

The Moderator of the General Assembly of the Church of Scotland Rev John H McIndoe, in his address in St Giles', spoke for the nation when he reflected that:

> *... during all the long pilgrimage of the years, the ideal of Scottish nationhood and the reality of Scottish identity have never been wholly obliterated from the hearts of the people. The recovery of this ancient symbol of the Stone cannot but strengthen the proud distinctiveness of the people of Scotland.*

THE KINGS AND QUEENS OF SCOTLAND

STEWART/STUART

1371–90	**Robert II**
1390–1406	**Robert III**
1406–37	**James I**
1437–60	**James II**
1460–88	**James III**
1488–1513	**James IV**
1513–42	**James V**
1542–67	**Mary Queen of Scots**[†]
1567–1625	**James VI**[‡]
1625–49	**Charles I**
1649–85	**Charles II**
1685–89	**James VII**
1689–94	**Mary II**
1689–1702	**William II**
1702–14	**Anne**

HANOVER

1714–27	**George I**
1727–60	**George II**
1760–1820	**George III**
1820–30	**George IV**
1830–37	**William IV**
1837–1901	**Victoria**

SAXE COBURG & GOTHA/WINDSOR

1901–10	**Edward VII**
1910–36	**George V**
1936	**Edward VIII**
1936–52	**George VI**
1952–	**Elizabeth II**

[†] executed 1589

[‡] also James I of England after Union of the Crowns in 1603

Places to Visit

Arbroath Abbey, Angus

The Stone of Destiny reappeared in the ruins of Arbroath Abbey in the spring of 1951, having been spirited out of Westminster Abbey a few months earlier. The location was deliberate – this was not the only time the abbey had been at the heart of Scottish history. In 1320, Scotland's nobles swore independence from England in a letter to the Pope – the Declaration of Arbroath. It famously reads: 'It is in truth not for glory, nor riches, nor honours that we are fighting, but for freedom – for that alone, which no honest man gives up but with life itself.' Founded in 1178, religious life in the abbey continued until the Protestant Reformation of 1560, following which parts of the abbey were dismantled.

Open daily April to September: 9.30am to 5.30pm
Open daily October to March: 10am to 4pm

DUNADD FORT, ARGYLL

This spectacular rocky outcrop in Kilmartin Glen was in use as a fort more than 2,000 years ago. It is one of the few places referenced in early histories, first mentioned in AD 683 when Dunadd was already a major power centre – possibly the chief stronghold of the kingdom of Dál Riata. Among the remarkable features still visible at Dunadd Fort today are two carved footprints. Potentially predecessors of the Honours and Stone of Destiny, these extraordinary symbolic carvings may have been used during inauguration ceremonies for new kings.

DUNNOTTAR CASTLE, ABERDEENSHIRE

The striking ruins of Dunnottar Castle perch on a cliff which stretches out into the North Sea. Once home to the powerful Earls Marischal, this castle played a vital role in the survival of the Honours – this is where they were taken for safekeeping when Oliver Cromwell invaded Scotland in 1650. The Honours were then buried at Kinneff Kirk further down the coast, which is also open to visitors. It is not known exactly when Dunnottar became a fortified site, but it was clearly a position of strength for hundreds of years. However, after the 10th Earl Marischal was convicted of treason in 1715 for his role in the first Jacobite uprising, the castle was seized then sold, with everything of value stripped out. It wasn't until the 1920s that restoration work was carried out and the castle opened to the public.

Open daily April to September: 9am to 5.30pm
Open daily October to March: 10am to various
(between 2.30pm to 4.30pm)

EDINBURGH CASTLE

This mighty fortress and former royal residence, with panoramic views of the city, is now a major part of the Old and New Towns of Edinburgh UNESCO World Heritage Site. Known as the 'defender of the nation', Edinburgh Castle is remarkable for many reasons, including being the location of Edinburgh's oldest building, the birthplace of James VI and the site of the Scottish National War Memorial. The Honours of Scotland and the Stone of Destiny are on display in the Crown Room. This is not merely the modern home of these historic objects – the Crown Room was created for the Honours around 1615, next to James VI's private apartment. It was in this room that they were sealed up following the Act of Union, only to be dramatically rediscovered one century later.

Open daily April to September: 9.30am to 6pm
Open daily October to March: 9.30am to 5pm

HOLYROOD ABBEY CHURCH AND THE PALACE OF HOLYROODHOUSE

Situated in the beautiful surrounds of Holyrood Park, Holyrood Palace and the roofless Holyrood Abbey have been linked with many royal lives. The abbey was founded by David I in 1128, although the walls still currently standing date from the early thirteenth century. Royal lodgings at the abbey gradually led to the development of the Palace of Holyroodhouse, the favoured home of royals in Scotland from the early sixteenth century. Today it is Queen Elizabeth II's official Scottish residence. The Honours have been transported down the Royal Mile to Holyrood Palace for notable ceremonies over the centuries. For an impression of Scottish royalty, both real and legendary (many have a connection with the Honours and Stone of Destiny), there are nearly one hundred portraits of monarchs hanging in the palace's Great Gallery.

Open daily April to October: 9.30am to 6pm
Open daily November to March: 9.30am to 4.30pm

Iona Abbey, Inner Hebrides

The tiny island of Iona has been a vibrant centre of Christian worship ever since St Columba arrived in AD 563. The monastery he founded was one of the most important and influential in the British Isles, and his fame attracted pilgrims from the seventh century onwards. Visitors today can follow a route similar to the Sràid nam Marbh ('Street of the Dead') taken by pilgrims of old, but it now ends at the restored thirteenth-century Iona Abbey, which stands on the site of Columba's church. It was Adomnán, Columba's biographer and successor as abbot, who first recorded the inauguration ceremony of a Scottish king when he looked back one hundred years to recount the story of Áedán mac Gabhráin being ordained by Columba.

Open daily April to September: 9.30am to 5.30pm
Open Monday to Saturday October to March: 10am to 4pm
Sundays unstaffed

St Giles' Cathedral, Edinburgh

The High Kirk of Edinburgh, St Giles' Cathedral, was founded in the twelfth century by King David I. The construction of the current building spanned many centuries and was the work of renowned craftspeople – the crown spire is an iconic landmark in the city skyline. With its pivotal position between Holyrood Palace and Edinburgh Castle, the church has often been central to Scottish religious – and consequently political – life, particularly during the Reformation in the sixteenth century. Among the many ceremonies to take place in this working church is the National Service of Thanksgiving, where the Honours are presented to new sovereigns.

Open daily May to September: Monday to Friday 9am to 7pm, Saturday 9am to 5pm, Sunday 1pm to 5pm
Open daily October to April: Monday to Saturday 9am to 5pm, Sunday 1pm to 5pm

Scone Palace, Perthshire

In the grounds of this stately home sits Moot Hill, the royal power centre where kings were inaugurated on the Stone of Destiny, a tradition reaching back to Pictish rulers. The twelfth-century Scone Abbey, founded by King Alexander I and used for coronations, once lay adjacent to Moot Hill. Even after the Stone was taken to England in the late thirteenth century under the command of Edward I of England, kings were crowned at Moot Hill as late as 1651, when Charles II was presented with the Honours as part of his coronation. Visitors to Scone can walk up Moot Hill, tour the grand nineteenth-century palace and explore the extensive grounds beside the River Tay, including the kitchen garden, maze and old graveyard.

Open daily May to September: 9.30am to 5pm (last admission)
Open daily March, April and October: 10am to 4pm (last admission)
November, December, February: grounds open on selected days 10am to 4pm (last admission)

SCOTTISH PARLIAMENT, EDINBURGH

The Crown of Scotland is taken from Edinburgh Castle to the State Opening of the Scottish Parliament every four years. At the inaugural State Opening in 1999, almost three hundred years had passed since the Scottish Parliament had last convened, after which the Honours had been consigned to a locked chest for two hundred years. Located at the bottom of the Royal Mile in the shadow of the Salisbury Crags, this unique building was designed by architect Enric Miralles to be 'sitting in the land'. Today the public can visit areas of the parliament building, take a guided tour, listen to introductory talks or reserve free tickets for Parliament debates and committee meetings.

Usually open to visitors Monday to Saturday 10am to 5pm, excluding the Christmas period and February recess.

Stirling Castle

As a consequence of its position on a vast volcanic rock at the meeting point between the Lowlands and Highlands, Stirling Castle was once the key to the kingdom of Scotland. Its origins are ancient and over the centuries it grew into a great royal residence, a commanding fortress and a symbol of Scottish national pride. Until the Union of the Crowns in 1603, the castle played a leading role in the lives of Scottish monarchs – including the crowning of the infant Mary Queen of Scots, the first to use the Crown, Sceptre and Sword of State we are familiar with today. When in Stirling there is also the opportunity to see the church where the coronation of Mary's son James VI took place – the Church of the Holy Rude. Generations of Scottish kings and queens have enlarged, adapted and embellished Stirling Castle, and visitors can follow in their footsteps.

Open daily April to September: 9.30am to 6pm
Open daily October to March: 9.30am to 5pm

IMAGE CREDITS

INDEX

HISTORIC ENVIRONMENT SCOTLAND

Historic Environment Scotland is the lead public body for Scotland's historic environment: a charity dedicated to the advancement of heritage, culture, education and environmental protection. We care for over three hundred properties across Scotland, actively record and interpret the nation's past, and hold the national record of architecture, archaeology and industry, a collection of over 5 million drawings, prints, maps, manuscripts and photographs.

Through our books, we are telling the stories of Scotland – exploring ideas and starting conversations about the past, present and future of our nation's history and heritage.

THE AUTHOR

Chris Tabraham is an archaeologist and historian. He worked for Historic Scotland for 40 years, first as Principal Inspector of Ancient Monuments and retiring as Principal Historian in 2010.